JEALOUS WITNESS

jealous witness

poems
by andrei codrescu

COFFEE HOUSE PRESS
Minneapolis
2008

COFFEE HOUSE PRESS books are available to the trade through our primary distributor, Consortium Book Sales & Distribution, www.cbsd.com or (800) 283-3572. For personal orders, catalogs, or other information, write to: Coffee House Press, 27 North Fourth Street, Suite 400, Minneapolis, MN 55401.

Coffee House Press is a nonprofit literary publishing house. Support from private foundations, corporate giving programs, government programs, and generous individuals helps make the publication of our books possible. We gratefully acknowledge their support in detail in the back of this book.

To you and our many readers around the world,
we send our thanks for your continuing support.

LIBRARY OF CONGRESS CIP INFORMATION
Codrescu, Andrei
Jealous witness : poems / by Andrei Codrescu.
p. cm.
Accompaning CD has the New Orleans Klezmer AllStars performing the poems.
ISBN 978-1-56689-217-9 (alk. paper)
1. Hurricane Katrina, 2005—Poetry. 2. New Orleans (La.)—Poetry.
1. New Orleans Klezmer AllStars. II. Title.
PS3553.03J43 2008
811'.54—DC22
2008012532

PRINTED IN THE UNITED STATES
3 5 7 9 8 6 4 2

JEALOUS WITNESS

before the storm: geographers in new orleans

maelstrom: songs of storm & exile

jealous witness

il maoismo (1971)

some poets

before the storm:
geographers in new orleans

before the storm: geographers in new orleans

Geographers must love being lost.
When a friend and colleague approached me
to speak to geographers I felt terror.
Speak to people who know where everything in the world is?
Who know north from south and east from west?
Who make the maps that were the bane of my school life,
though I appreciated them for the aesthetic works that many of
    them were?
People who generation after generation filled in the terra
    incognitas
until the only blank spaces left on maps were ones that had the
misfortune—or good sense—to change their locations—or at least
    their names—after cataclysmic events?

But then I thought that it must
be a terribly frustrating profession
given the constant intrusions of nature on the topography of a
    changing earth
        and the intrusions of history on what's there one minute and
                gone the next
the superimposition of boundary lines made by men
over those of nature and the migratory life that follows nature's
    lines
and the intrusions as well of our ontological and psychological
    understanding
of where we are at any given moment
with or without maps.

Maps go against common sense.
Even the most skilled readers of maps know they are
performing an unnatural act that is in itself an intrusion on the
    natural and human world.
The makers of maps already know this
and the venality that lies at the base of all that codified
exploration and so-called "discovery."
One could write a book, and I'm sure many have been
    written
on the ethics of mapping.
Geographers must be like Mormons
always endeavoring for accuracy and precision
in order to correct some egregious flaw in the founding.
This made them energetic and restless people buffeted
by the storm of profound dilemmas brought about by shaky
    beginnings.

My own beginning was shaky
born in a place drawn and redrawn after every war
a ping-pong region batted about by great powers
settled at the time of my birth inside the fish of Romania
"Our country looks like a fish," saith my geography teacher
with an indescribable irony that carried in it some unspoken curse
of something slippery, silent, ready to be hooked by the many
fishermen hovering above us with various maps spread before
    them
I made my own maps
pirate maps leading to treasures
secret maps for our gang's secret places
maps for getting to my house
and escape maps in case of a bad oedipal storm
I realized then that the treasure map and the escape map
    were ur-maps

the first drawn to locate the loot
the second intended to escape the armed looters
and that the fine humanist sentiment of discovery
was mostly an ode-for-hire to legitimize
the taking of treasure and the necessity of escape
I knew this even at ten because I wanted to go to new places
and discover worlds unknown to me
just like all the poetry said
but I was principally motivated by the desire to escape
the tight borders of my walled-in childhood in a walled-in country
in a walled-in continent and a walled-in prison planet
and there is surely a book to be written and many have
on the imaginary geography of childhood
and imaginary geography before the age of physical discovery
and the rise of instrumentation
I still have notebooks full of detailed description
of places on my imaginary maps.

Imaginary geography is still the prime mover
of human beings now when all that can be seen and measured
has been seemingly mapped seen and measured
and that far from being exhausted or literary
this particular imagination is reshaping our world
making it necessary to re-envision its mapping according to desire

And there is no better time for discussing this mapping of desire
than the day after Mardi Gras in New Orleans
with the storm-tossed souls of geographers
in the de facto reality of this American Venice
perilously submerged by the wine-dark sea of professional
    doubts
or so I like to think.
I mean why practice a profession if not for the purpose of doubting

mine never had any other purpose
but then it might not be a profession at all
it's certainly not a career
driving people crazy.
So, geographers, I commend you for being in this
city that refuses to conform to anything that is known about it
and has had its geography redrawn and reimagined
first as a creature of the lower mississippi
a river that has no intention of conforming and never has
to the designs of those that'd fix its course and propensities
a city founded against common sense in a hostile swamp
then fought over by the great powers of Europe
the subject of countless imprecise descriptions and claims
a city where geographical directions such as north west south east
    are not part of the natives' map
who give directions as either "away" or "toward" the river
and whose boundaries and life have been re-imagined many times
by the life-forms that stubbornly thrive here
waging a guerrilla war against definition and conclusive mapping
and will continue to do so until the city is either taken back or
    abandoned
        by the river
a knowledge of finitude that is intimately woven into our psyches
and that urges us to live intensely before the assured cataclysm
a tenuous and time-bound existence that gives an infinite license
    to the imagination
the infinite by the way is available only to the tragic sense of
    existence
    which makes us all wine-dark kierkegardians.

I will use four concepts drawn from my fellow writers to give you a
    particular
sense of this region
good hopefully for revisionings of anyplace:

These are:
Proprioception or *Charles Olson's Poetics*
Mysteries
Surregionalism
& *T.A.Z.*

Proprioception or *Olson's Poetics*, as developed by Olson in his long
poem, "Maximus," and his essays on Melville, "Human Universe," and
"Projective Verse," at the end of the 1950s.

Charles Olson's vision of American space was embodied by his home-
town of Gloucester, Massachussetts, and was a simultaneous cosmic,
geological, human, economical, political, psychological, and literary
exploration by means of a poetic method he called "projective verse,"
driven by proprioception, which is a synesthesic drive to compress and
push forward all that one knows and intuits in that knowledge as well
as in imagination. Olson envisioned Gloucester as a becoming out of
known facts, a journey that the poet undertakes as a twentieth-cen-
tury Odysseus who has been schooled in everything since Homer.

Of course, that's an epic undertaking that can lead to madness, as
Olson himself acknowledged: *"What did happen to measure when the
rigidities dissolved? . . . What is measure when the universe flips and no
part is discrete from another part except by the flow of creation, in and out,
intensive where it seemed before qualitative, and the extensive exactly the
widest, which we have also the powers to include?"*

This postmodern vision looks to me exactly like the Mississippi River seen both before and after "discovery," and there are many poets, local and not local, who've tried to make their work approximate that great force, intuiting rather than describing it. Such a project comes out of a profound mistrust toward the official readings of one's habitation. As a poet, Olson was not satisfied by the results of the modern critiques of Marx and Freud because, while they seemingly overthrew the official readings, they produced equally dogmatic and official readings of their own. The modern ideologies did not open the space of Gloucester (or of thought, or of the Mississippi) to the unknown, but enclosed it instead within their own logic. Olson's poetics made simultaneous use of contradictory readings. Olson may have even coined the term "postmodern"—and pointed out the way to a revisioning of place. What makes reading Olson difficult is that the reader is never given quite enough space to reinvision the poet's revisioning —Olson knew too much and he laid it all out in a cinematic sort of way that only the hippest movie buffs can truly enjoy—accustomed as they are now to quick cuts and montage.

Mysteries as revealed in *The Mysteries of New Orleans* by Baron von Reizenstein, completed in 1853, translated and edited by Steven Rowan, The Johns Hopkins University Press, 2002.

Baron von Reizenstein, a young German aristocrat, was sent to New Orleans by his parents in the mid-nineteenth century in the hope that he wouldn't get mixed up in Germany's revolutionary ferment. So, instead of becoming a European radical, he came to pre-Civil War New Orleans and found a place that was in a state of ferment far beyond the anti-oedipal socialism of Germany—it was putrefact, in fact, fermenting both literally and metaphorically. It was a multicultural, decadent mix of the new and old world, a psychological laboratory, a wide-open port. A thriving German community supported two German-language newspapers, a Bohemian one and a proper one. The young Baron wrote *The Mysteries of New Orleans* in German as a serial in the *Louisiana Staat-Zeitung*, the Bohemian paper. By 1850 the genre of "The Mysteries of . . ." was well-established in the New World by German writers; there were already *The Mysteries of Cleveland* and *The Mysteries of Pittsburgh*. The genre itself was born of Eugène Sue's *The Mysteries of Paris*, a brilliant re-envisioning of one's own city as an exotic locale. Sue, who was too poor to travel, turned an awed gaze to the familiar and gave his readers a city they would recognize but which hid a poetry far from the familiar. Von Reizenstein saw New Orleans as a place of infinite possibilities, but also as a great unwritten and continually unfolding experiment. He described, daringly and possibly for the first time here, lesbian and homosexual love, and gave every street in the city an essential character and a stage for activities that were only partly imagined and that are true to this day. Reizenstein was an abolitionist who was able to render unselfconsciously the complex relationships between slaves and masters, a rogue who loved shocking his readers with the sexual shenanigans of the city, a reformer who described vividly a profound corruption that's still, alas, part of the city's fabric. His contemporary readers doubtlessly recognized their city and, because of it, they stayed when Reizenstein took them abruptly into a world of magic and horror that had its source in the yellow fever epidemic, and introduced characters with superhuman powers. The yellow fever itself was spread through the seeds of a psychedelic plant found at the source of the Red River. A magical weave of African ritual and Christian superstition superimposes its geography on that of the "real" New Orleans. Reading von Reizenstein now one is seized suddenly by the certainty of the existence of this magical geography in our time. I certainly was, because, long before reading *The Mysteries of New Orleans,* I wrote a book called *Messiah,* which takes place in this city and introduces a magical cast and a mystical geography that coincides more than eerily with Reizenstein's one hundred years earlier. I am not the only one. With various degree of skill, dozens of writers, including Anne Rice, have stumbled on the same secrets or mysteries of New Orleans, that vibrational reality that lies like gossamer over its physical features and permeates even the most casual visitor with a strange sense of something invisible.

In *A River and Its City: The Nature of Landscape in New Orleans*, by Ari Kelman, University of California Press, a book that I opened at random, I found this: "*Yellow fever emptied some spaces and filled others, redefining the way New Orleans used and viewed their public landscapes.*" The author goes on to write, "*cities and surroundings should not be seen in opposition to each other. Instead we find the built and the natural mingling as part of the complex narrative of New Orleans' urban-environmental history.*"

And, I might add, its supernatural history.
To me this means that: 1) New Orleans has specific Geniuses of the Locus, local deities present in the geography before its founding, who grew and grow increasingly more specific in place and time, neither one of which stands still, and 2) New Orleans is imaginable, hospitable to the geography of desires that anyone can project imaginatively on it, finding the appropriate receptors without much difficulty. It's a party town.

Surregionalism, as coined by the philosopher Max Cafard, first published in *Exquisite Corpse, a Journal of Life & Letters*, 1997.

Max Cafard's Surregionalism. I quote: "*Where is the Region anyway? For every Logic there is a Region. To mention those of particular interest to us, the Surregionalists: Ecoregions, Georegions, Psychoregions, Mythoregions, Ethnoregions, Socioregions, and Bioregions. Regions are inclusive. They have no borders, no boundaries, no frontiers, no State Lines. Though Regionalists are marginal, Regions have no margins. Regions are traversed by a multitude of lines, folds, ridges, seams, pleats. But all lines are included, none exclude. Regions are bodies. Interpenetrating bodies. Interpenetrating bodies in semi-simultaneous spaces. (like Strangers in the Night.)*"

What use maps here? You might as well throw them away now, especially those provided by the Tourism Bureau.

In Surregionalism we have a vision of New Orleans as a place both emptied by its geography and history to accommodate new bodies and reimaginings, and a creative matrix that is a near-perfect rhizome, an über-potato. It is also a uniquely well-developed matrix poised to serve as a model for other city-regions. It may be too late for some cities that have been destroyed by overplanning, too radical a separation from the surrounding environment, too much "economic development," overpriced real estate, and so-called "community standards," which, in most places, mean the institution of deadly silence by mean old men. It is not too late in regions founded on generative paradoxes, such as Salt Lake City—paradoxically.

Our paradox is carnival—*carne vale*—farewell to the flesh—and we say quite a farewell here. The mysteries of New Orleans participate in the surregional world as fully empowered tentacles.

Which is not to say that we are not threatened with a loss of eternity, like everyone else in the world. Because of this threat, we resort, like all magical souls the world over, to fast-moving, nomadic vehicles called T.A.Z., or Temporary Autonomous Zones.

& *T.A.Z.*, Temporary Autonomous Zones, coined by the Sufi scholar and poet Hakim Bey, who discussed T.A.Z. in a number of essays, including a slim volume published and reprinted several times by Autonomedia in the mid-nineties.

T.A.Z. exist almost everywhere and can show up anywhere, because they are nomadic, but they are particularly fond of New Orleans because it is the most T.A.Z.-hospitable city in America and, consequently, some of our T.A.Z. have become nearly sedentary.

T.A.Z. are only successful as long as they are nomadic. They can only stay in place as long as they fly below radar. T.A.Z. take root in poor areas of cities or the unincorporated countryside where space is plentiful and there are mixed cultures. Tazzerites thrive in racially and culturally diverse environments from which they draw the strength to grow, but then they are noticed, and this eventually draws scouts, geographers, and zoning. These are followed by land-development, rising real-estate prices, city planning, preservation societies, law enforcement, and art simulacra. The lifespan of T.A.Z. used to be decades-long until the last quarter of the twentieth century when T.A.Z. destruction accelerated, making T.A.Z. short-lived and prone to extinction, but also smaller, faster, and harder to spot. Tazzerites draw their territorial lines through song and dance like the native Australians. Tazzerites use local concepts of time and space that they activate with found materials, speak a variety of hipster lingos, and use advanced technology to communicate. The "objects" they make are temporal and ephemeral but they transcend time and space to link both vertically through history and horizontally through geography with all T.A.Z. past and present. They are connected to each other across the globe and often merge when one of them is destroyed.

I call the T.A.Z. of New Orleans Narcississipi, because it is in Louisiana cradled by the Mississippi. Narcississippi is under attack by powerful image-making conglomerates and aggressive zoning, but, for the time being, we still man the night shift in New Orleans.

Perhaps you have gotten at least a little lost.
It was my intention.
The figure of the lost geographer is an archetype.
I'm sure that Rabelais would have loved it.
I certainly do.

—2004

maelstrom:
songs of storm & exile

did something miss new orleans?

what do you call this this catastrophe sonnet
used to be called n'awrleans now it's simply
the greatest engineering disaster in u.s. history
before that it was the greatest human disaster
in pre-civil war history the place to sell slaves
who misbehaved downriver and before that
the greatest rum sugar and human warehouse
in north america the end of the pipe out of which
poured sweet drunkenness and blood and patois
from martinique through the pirate spanish main
before that it was just the greatest swamp a drunk
frenchman ever dedicated to his sun king
so let's rebuild this with new urban principles
that bow to history without throwing up

the wind family
the insurance company question: wind or water?

severe weather and powerlines down
rain and powerlines and all our representatives
are busy powerlines feeding the call-waiting
of millions breathing in the dark a big animal
called the gulf coast a heavy wet mammal
getting its fins back from the genetic storeroom
now where did we put that was it with the wings
look they aren't rotten like all the meat
in the moonlit fridges lining the grand boulevards
and streets named Music Humanity and Melpomene
with graffiti *do not open cheney and rice inside*
chem trails are real . . . secret CIA prison inside
once there was a house here I lived in it
there was deer meat in the fridge and fish
and two dead ducks and a whole box of x-mas pears
courtesy of our people the winds

fridges to heaven

under the silver moonlight
fridges line the street
far as the eye can see
they are still full of meat
more toxic than you and me
dick cheney inside
and president bush too
and that FEMA guy too
tape them doors shut
so they won't come after us
full of maggots and good news
frigidaires all up the avenue
where the big trees used to be
I used to keep my champagne chilled
steaks and chocolate too
and a couple of frozen dinners
for those late nights on Decatur
now it looks like every other
fridge on the avenue
just a number in a nameless row
under the silver moonlight

the mold song

it was one of a kind
the earliest map of the united states
it was hanging right here on the wall
the mold ate it all
in one gulp the mold ate it all
and these books the only copies
of newton franklin galileo
and this shakespeare folio
the mold ate them like they was candy
look at the satisfied grinning mold
stretching from floor to floor
like a fifties horror movie mold
not to speak of that stack of cash
I never shoulda kept around
not a zero left in the whole stack
look at me I'm growing old
I'm giving myself to the mold
it's some kind of lesson
it's some kind of horror story
keep collecting paper things
I knew that one day I'd be sorry
I'm not wearing a mask
I'm not wearing any gloves
I feel stupid I feel cold
I'm giving myself to the mold
halloween and suicide rolled in one

I shoulda sold I shoulda sold
only in new orleans only in new orleans
halloween and suicide all in one
a man of means

what to do with your goat in a drowning world

hear the helicopters come over the roof
water's up to my attic windows
and I'm stuck here with my goat
I can see my neighbor in the hole on his roof
he's got two dachsies and a tomcat
just across the rushing river is his sister
she's cradling her baby and a rooster
circling helicopters circling helicopters
will take me but not my goat
will lift me up from muck and flood
but they won't take my neighbor's dogs or cat
or his sister's baby's rooster
helicopters overhead nation to the rescue
take the people damn their friends
I'm not going without my goat
he's not going without his pets
baby won't leave without her rooster
lord oh lord why don't we have an ark
that's the helicopters leaving
that's the nation to the rescue
leaving us here in the dark

looting wal-mart

they looted wal-mart and they took the rifles
they looted wal-mart and they took the diapers
they looted wal-mart and they took the drapes
they looted wal-mart and they took the baby formula
we gotta be tough we gotta be tough
send in the national guard do we have enough
soldiers do we have enough soldiers
half of them are in iraq
but we've got the other half they just landed here
they took their positions they are ready to shoot
look at them crouching ready for combat
who they gonna combat who they gonna combat
two days ago two days ago
they already looted the wal-mart
they looted wal-mart and they took the rifles
they looted wal-mart and they took the baby formula
if they come back to loot wal-mart they gonna find the guard
yeah the guard ready to shoot
how quickly they forgot how hard everybody fought
against putting in this wal-mart
how quickly they forgot how they didn't want a wal-mart here
but now that they've looted wal-mart
we want the national guard here
they've looted wal-mart and took everybody's memory
they've looted wal-mart and left us our history

the coffee house philosophers

we are the hard-working middle class
we're mortgaged up to our ass
we paid your taxes fought for better schools
spoke loud so that they'd pave our streets
we staffed your downtown buildings
filled your restaurants and made your nightlife
new orleans new orleans our vanished city
we sit in coffee houses telling our stories over 'n' over
like crickets in the summer grass
we'll flee from you like bees from dying clover
we are your vanished middle-class new orleans
we are your coffee house philosophers waiting
for our ticket out of here
chewing the cud and mixing metaphors
only the very rich and their servants will remain
when we flee your storm-tossed shores new orleans
you have lost your middle class
woe is unto you city of under-upper class
you played at feudal pageants and we laughed
but now you are feudal and we cry

let's watch my house float
(or, lawyers having p.t.s.d. sex)

I met a lawyer in the street
usually it's hey hey I gotta go
or you owe me that dinner you know
but now it's hey can you drive me
to lakeview to see my house rot
sure why not
let's drive to lakeview
to see where your house used to float
and then to the ninth to see everybody's houses rot
and then let's have some drinks on the levee
like you wasn't my lawyer who took everything I got
when I sued my broker for overbuying techs
that was the nineties so long long ago
let's watch the river flow we got nothing else to do
then let's have p.t.s.d. sex
start everything from scratch

mother quarter

acquaintances greet each other
friends that haven't seen each other in ages
strangers meet strangers
the bars are full the parking scarce
how is your house darlin
how is your life and your mementos
your tchotchkes and your mother
it's gone I'm gone but he or she is fine
mostly I seem to be alive
it's dark where I'm staying
so I came to the Quarter
there is nothing where I used to live
so I'm crashing in the Quarter now
I drove four hundred miles to be here
it's the old hood the old ship
by the quiet thank G-d Mississip
I've pulled away from the USA
and set my anchor in the Quarter
right here in *la vie en rose café*
I feel the dead around me who in times past
came right here and sat in the coffee house
and tried to think of what came next
something always did
some conspired to make money
others wrote kvetched or hid
something always came next

in 1812 in 1850 1956 1968
main thing is we are still alive
here in the old french quarter
can you believe it's 2005
in the old french mother ship

the town meeting

mr mayor I knew your mama
don't you do me wrong
tell me now when I can go home
mr mayor we went to school together
you broke the rules I didn't tell
when they gonna give us back the light and gas
mr mayor I voted for you
and all my people knew your people
when they gonna say what we can do
mr mayor I sang at your party and all my children too
when they gonna send those checks
remember I voted for you
mr mayor mr mayor we were born here
played here made it through our teens
we are men and women now
when can we have back our new orleans
mr mayor mr mayor tell the president
get that governor and officials in d.c.
to do something for me
where you going mr mayor

tale of two cities

this is a tale of two cities
that didn't even speak each others' names
before the deluge
one was empty big and pretty
the other poor proud loud and artsy
but that was before the deluge
when the waters joined them
and made new orleans in baton rouge

now long before the waters rose
one man only ever made the trip
from new orleans to baton rouge
he was from the confederacy of dunces
his name was ignatius and he said
don't go there it's full of yokels
there is a phallus-shaped tower
and the hicks hate us city slicks
they have all the power high and low
don't you ever go there no no no
they have empty roads and big huge houses
in that hicksville baton rouge
we've got us characters and civilization
our cathouses and bars are known in all the nation
but that was before the deluge
when we redefined civilization
they welcomed us in baton rouge

they didn't chase our orphans from their tower
they let us cram their roads with cars
they opened wide their big huge houses
they filled our scripts for tranquilizers
they made us feel that we were one
big confederacy of dunces
they made new orleans in baton rouge
after the deluge

the breakups

o the married men's girlfriends
o the girlfriends of married men!
she's in houston I'm in philly
o it kills me to be here with my wife's large family
o it kills me to be here with my exes and their brood
o it kills me that it's monday and I'm watching bad tv
I could be in new orleans listening to the rain
just you and me just you and me
o the rain was bad enough o the wind was horrific
I'm back in the straight world feeling silly
he's in houston I'm in philly
back where we ran from the big family
everything seems way back then
o the married men's girlfriends!
o the girlfriends of married men!
I'm not with you I am with them
the wind was bad enough I have no home
and your cell phone doesn't work

from the window at molly's

it's just like old times for a minute
gossip rumors innuendo
can I buy you another drink
the city's coming back I feel it
it's back right now don't you think
then I look out Molly's window
where the Quarter girls go by on bikes
the fresh flowers of the Vieux Carré
tattooed like sailors on a spree
and I see only contractors and soldiers
tough hombres and country boys
not a fleur among them as they stroll
casing up a made-up gal with dollar signs
in her hard hard eyes set to no
where did all the fresh flowers go
where did all the Quarter gals disappear
where are the tattoos of yesteryear

that fema check

black friday came and cyber monday too
dahlin all of america was in the malls
I saw everybody there looking like you'd expect
after a wreck
it was fun to see us all and hear everyone say
I see you got that FEMA check!
my house is gone and I've been here
where they have such shopping malls
we never saw in new orleans
people here are kind and full of x-mas cheer
as they max their credit cards
let's join them let bygones be bygones
we looking pretty good after the wreck
I see you got your FEMA check!

crepuscular (the family tomb)

bodies in the flood
just like in the days of noah
cemeteries rising
the dead are coming back
but no saints are marching in
Is that my body in the flood
no cause I'm not poor and black
stubborn crazy or sentimental
but it sure looks like the dead are coming back
it sure looks like a bad moon rising
bodies in the flood
just like in the days of noah
with nobody to pick them up
just like in the days of FEMA

cleaning ladies

they were cleansing storms
katrina and rita
they were cleaning women
hired by the housing boom broom
real estate real estate
you kept rising like the water
but the poor kept staying on
in the days before the storms
then came katrina and rita
to finish what you began
cleansing storms oh cleaning ladies
making realtor dreams come true
oh look over that rising sea
I'll take the lobster and the vino
see the shining shining city
it's the new new orleans rising
coin-operated by casinos

new orleans limbo

when it happens all of a sudden
it takes a while to realize you're dead
you keep eating that étoufée
wondering why it don't get any smaller
you keep talking to your friends
amused by their look of instant horror
you keep running that commercial
urging folks to make their reservations
come early and stay late
you keep posting all those deals
this is the best real estate
the best for all eternity
it takes a while to realize you're dead
this is eternity
when it happens just like that

postscript to a prequel

In New Orleans Jews join the Krewe de Jew
And throw glittery bagels instead of beads to the mob
The Mardi Gras bagel is the Jewish Zulu coconut
Don't tell your mamele what the girls do for the grab
In New Orleans Jews lament the hexed Saints
And wear paper bags on their heads at football games
If God willing the team makes it to the playoffs
the rebbe leads the congregation through the streets
playing When the Saints Come Marching In on the shofar
In New Orleans the Jews listen to the blues
In New Orleans Jews listen to the jazz
In New Orleans the Jews will sometimes eat ribs
In New Orleans some Jews will eat red bugs
In New Orleans the Jews put honey in their grits
In New Orleans Jews run for mayor and Carnival royalty
It's known that Judah P. Benjamin was Vice President of the Confederacy
and Elvis was a shabbas goy
In New Orleans Jews fear only amnesia

The New Orleans Klezmer AllStars recorded this poem before the Storm.
It is not included in the enclosed CD, *which contains only Katrina songs.*

jealous witness

in the picture above

the graduating class of 1927
portland women's college stands in expectation
of the jazz age above the bed together
with a full deck of your female ancestors
jealous witness of our lovemaking or just
your hello to the past and sorry girls
the thirties are just ahead not that we know
much better what the teens of the 21st hold

—(for Laura)

the idiot at the front desk

why do you think I'm at the front desk
the tattooed genius they've got in the back
and buried right under *his* feet is god
they have a technique these guys
they believe in the meritocracy of the first impression
the most beautiful woman in the village
draws spectators not just customers
spectators are future customers who feed
on her looks to make themselves richer
to be worthy of her to make her surrender herself to them
and when she does they close their eyes
and when they open them they are holding the genius
from the back in their arms and he speaks with an accent
god squirms under the ground and a new consuming class
is born to his whooping delight
out of which he fashions a slew of new front desk idiots
and so does beauty spread skin-deep in offices and on screens

the nose with no dialogue
with laura june 6 2003 over america

virginia nicole wolf kidman's nose hangs over our heads as the plane shoves
over the
    continental divide
and the computer keys feel funky from too much typing
      you're on vacation enough already
    the vermin are massing on schopenhauer
I explain to my fomer student now a movie attorney
      in the seat across the isle:
the language *the mysteries of new orleans* was written in was german
    I feel the urge so I must act on it & I do even as the woman with
formica breasts
    holds a coffee cup toward virginia nicole's nose at thirty thousand feet
of pure airplane air & the sweat of thousands of people now safely
    on the ground
      some of them getting their noses fixed
and the sweat of the three hundred or so sweating right now & breathing
    through their average noses
or weeping extraordinary purple tears in their ordinary houses watching
    laparoscopic
      surgery on the learning channel
we learn for instance that cleavage should be balanced front and back
    by a tiny set of dumbbells trip-wired to nipples
      hardened by a sneezing
dwarf waving a bouquet of dandruffed pony hairs back and forth in front
    of the subjects

under discussion!
we're over Arizona for sure now that's the desert baby it's all eroded
    and we're
        only halfway there half eroded
the proboscis of an old volcano purring under us like a softened periscope
    so many colors pink and everything
I've missed while typing
    you're cruel and Meryl Streep is crying & wiping her real
        nose on her pretend apron she's miserable!
but she has and always will have "precious memories among the clouds,"
    just like us

topiary

"There are four kinds of people: those who have not been born, those who are living, those who have died, and those who have not been born, are not living and have not died. They are the stars." —mircea cărtărescu

and those who are blossoming in the brain
of a child over and over
born of an understanding
that will not recur after age fifteen but will be forever true
imaginary people with some very good and some very bad traits
many of them with a black eyepatch and peg-leg but always on your side
sometimes these people have to cluster to disguise themselves
in a mercury mushroom holding its form
a bloom that chooses a photographic process to become invisible
a heart that will not stop emitting rays of hurt and healing
a mouth murmuring enchantments toward its own self.
Then at fifteen the prison bars become articulate,
the masked arabesques harden into architectures
oozing soft knowledge, facts, and emphasis.
I've been working on not forgetting
it's no child's play looking all grown up and fooling everybody
gombrowicz was right and so were many other goombas
looks are everything disregard them.
The pall descends the pail fills from the deepening well,
time is a racket that swings at the tennis balls of truth,
a wasp nest grows thick with the buzzing
of ten million wasps sounding like new york city.

A deaf bear in a forest cave licks a memory from his paw,
there is a thickness in everything skin grows muted over skin.
They've tacked you like a fabric to the dummy they call reality,
unsnapping yourself is no picnic.
The logos of unfastening churns unrecorded.
The face of a benevolent taurine cloud plays over field
just over the horizon it's death and her gallant ten thousand
(fleas, motes, eyes?)
driving the motorized galaxy toward you,
the one slowpoke in the streaming data stream.
The palliatives of transcendence are the business
of the young who think they know from the screens in their pockets
just who it is they know better than you
all those black-patched peg-legged people on their side
you used to know from books and from nowhere
but the screens know them better than they know
and these people may be another species altogether
a whole other kind of people who promise much.
They will get universes of nothing for little money.
When a line of verse escapes the open wallet
it heads straight for the sky to bag a passing angel
just doing its job buffing a tired star.
The young in the pixel dust are gratified
that the old in their fugitive nobility of ashes
have taken their stories with them.
Those would have been way too heavy.
The unborn people are just around the corner.

WITOLD GOMBROWICZ (1904-1969) was born in Poland, spent most of his life in exile in Argentina, and died in Venice. He wrote *Ferdydurke*, about a grown-up who wakes up in high school in the body of a teenager, and finds himself unable, despite major philosophical and physical attempts, to prove that he doesn't belong there. English translation by Danuta Borchardt.

visitors from the dancing world

the dancers we are about to meet
are fourteen thousand and twenty thousand years old
but look fourteen in their frayed satin slippers no hips round eyes
they have danced a number of universes some of which have exploded
and tender others just being powered for use by life forms like ours
they visit us because we are one of their earlier creations
they don't use the door they come in the window
or like last time through a crack in the roof
that time they rested their pergament wings
(the same book bindings are made from)
and danced shut doors trapdoors exits so it would be just them and us
we clunky in felt boots with ice chunks in eyebrows keyboards in hand
histories accounts tacked neatly on walls of empty space we did these things
and these things thousands of years are a long time to wait for the dancers
the dancing wu ling masters the sentient motes with skins of brilliant dust
but here they are the darkened air crackles our eyes half-closed taste red
a long time ago their god diaghilev assured them that as long as they
believed in him he would be a window into the lights of the sky and a roof
over their heads a master of luminous dots infusing them with power

as long as they never use the door never never use the door
because he explained eons ago he was a ball of such energy
anyone coming into his house using a door would be incinerated
from his rocker he always faced the door
waiting for trespassers with his umbilical cord plugged in
the sadness of the kind of god I am

he explained cannot be explained
but stick to this simple rule of ingress and egress
and I'll keep you light and fluffy except for those wings
those I have to fashion from pergament
and he wiggled his umbilical and emitted pas de deux and jetées
and now as we flatten in expectation like pages from our favorite books
as his angels fly in, in tight formations of v and Q &
the vanguard are in violet followed by bright carmine and azure
the violet carry two carmines on their backs pulled by one azure
by a thread of gold unraveling behind them
followed by a gaggle of black-clad immigrants from Ellis Island
with steel-weighted suitcases and hearts in canvas sacks
though in fairness some of them have a bubble of happy air
bouncing off a drumskin in their chest so they are already in jerusalem
as unpacked as the dancers no longer heavy with the past
we flatten in expectation of them like pages from our favorite books
they are a crowd with verses trailing them wherever they go
medieval banners unscrolled behind angels in paintings
when we sit down to eat this evening it is for them we fill wineglasses
and we thank them as they land clumsily on the trees and the deck
even when they fail their designated spots they still carry enough otherness
to assure everyone that they and we are not alone that thousands of beings
in flight and in states of luminosity are just a few inches behind and ahead
their heat is generous and communal their bodies slender and available
they are us in our youth and you in yours time hasn't passed
time took some of the others now they are back illuminated
this old age you can have it tonight the landing party lands

walnuts

"I don't like the substances from which poetry is made: smells too much like ether, like nail polish. You have to consume your own self too much. . . . The true prose writer consumes others." —mircea cărtărescu

other than remembering what was designed for forgetting
which is everything even you and other musical works
intended to get your own music going your architecky self
brilliantly described in vast oeuvre of wishful thinking
intended as well as brilliant lagniappe for conquest of others
your nose drinks in the *désuet* perfumes of early works
not so *désuet* as all that in re-reading rather active
an angry youth throwing flaming bombs at passing metaphorists
savonarolaishly flinging to hell deniers of other realities
even boring realities identical to ours at moments of actual ennui
the defense of sound distortion through the larynx
of even the least talented a great cause a flag to plant in magma
not a shred of nostalgia anywhere just manly jobs
war demolition damsel-flipping crystal pedagogy aphorism
some of it sloppy broken eggs etc but the sun on the hill city etc
the operations we now see on the big map and admire for strategy
well not really there wasn't any except forward (man) for Poetry
frothed head to foot in spume and steel of youth
then time showed up and the game had a referee a pudgy dude
not that I really cared to find out what I'd done or said
that was all battle and in war all is fair and bloody pink
but I read my contemporaries for clues about the weather

there was clearly more weather than we saw on tv
there were whole countries of weather where a giant cardiogram
was being constructed from the heartbeats of millions hoping for something
there were forests being devoured and air becoming carbon
misshapen channels embodied to broadcast doom that wouldn't leave
even familiar gestures and salutes were clouds of strange
try as you/I/it might you/I or it couldn't make history by ourselves
toys played by the wind are eerie no matter how clever they are
my brilliant contemporaries inscribed mercury drops with scents
that were libraries to dogs who didn't teach them to the hounds of hell
(we did that through metaphor and school)
dogs rolled scents and clues down squiggly country roads
where apotheosis in the shape of a coffee cup rewarded the tired
the sun ahead in the rain-wipers through muted cheers of dying
sometimes cheerleaders in the raindrops caught snacking
audible in the steady rain crunch crunch white teeth
dazzling details of inimitable childhoods looking sadly
similar from inches away that was sad but heck there were colors
gypsy skirts gleeful snotty brats lacquer-shiny bugs in oily rainbows
the terrorists have won by now so kill yourself
the fog is creepy nostalgia the shells thankfully still from lemuria
the world is littered with bodies left behind by you/it/I
who kill selves in more places more times more lines
than I count presently either in your forehead or in the sketch
of the town from above by a fine dutch master each line made of lines
until the field under the cathedral is populated by peasants
and those other shapes are coffins or boats I believe or dragons
with chinese lanterns between their spines like mirabeau bridge
the peasants pop their blossoms or time capsules over their heads
or maybe hats who knew that hats could be such historians
and among all that action the stick figures of museum curators
they aren't yet born but already are very busy collecting
nits and mots from poet stripped thin in walnut covered shore

ars poetica (candles and lepidoptera)

live as if you were art and had other purposes
than just living and you might or might not make it
it's a rough neighborhood better move to (blank)
there aren't any places like that anymore
except in your head, the new boho quarter—
here are ten things I will never tell anybody:
about the time when incident #
about that place where we this and there—
you can also make art out of other peoples' lives
but you can't let them know that—
darling today I will take the fine flour of your day
and bake a loaf of bread from it—
or, I'm not telling you this but the sushi dinner
you are so enjoying is made from the crude observations
you made during this strange and stormy week—
the impulse to show yourself naked is to inner truth
what the mask is to the average new orleanian—
bad poetry is where each line announces things
that will not be named—this could be a very bad poem—
the air was white milky chalky the baby-powder factory blew up—
henry kissinger proves you can get tall women to beat
your pudgy face with their breasts sincerely while by the side
of the road an empty police cruiser scares the out-of-towners—
the real police are in bars doing coke in the bathroom—
everybody's dying for art come in my mouth and call me names—
a vague religious culture both prevents and hastens the end—

cruel tapestry, arabs, etc—from lowbrow to kitsch in one effortless
click, and time-travel, too—tv perpetually tuned to the retraction channel—
a man hears a story and sees his naked daughter in the sauna—
she is steaming with young republicans and old derelicts—neo-neo—
live as a neoclassical thing a cascade of simplicity—
I am a blue-lipped businessman hiding from the cold behind
a monroe-hipped escort in a tight red dress and fuck-me-pumps—
my tie is not askew—
I hope that people like me even though there is so much of me—
on the smoke-darkened ceiling runs a carved wooden serpent—
the use-value of things in a novel is different from a shopping mall—
take creatures (nonshoppers) and group them by lostness
on porch and field—never put a question mark
where god has put a period—my only advice and I'm proffering it
through a set of antique speakers is: listen to what you just said!
(wrote—sang—hung in the window)—
the bartender's name is mr. tiger who knows all the songs—
he is a new being half old wino half hipster and something blue—
his old lady at the bar dissects oxford england 1964—
form is form, ok? the late great planet earth—rapture-faust insurance—
we are from the jewish conspiracy—and the society for the study
of immortality—each letter is an atom—by manipulating your letters
we can preserve you indefinitely or until such time as the middle ages
are shipped to britain—
having once taken refuge in writing I know the way it works:
newt-harvested foreskins are glued to the pupils' eyelids—
when they wake up they speak of two seas of language:
the written and the buzzed—"every girl a contortionist!"
it's the only lesbian reference in the bible. (romans 2)
us and them I think—

arse poetica 2: the art of restraint

The Arse of Restraint.
I practice it.
Tell others nothing.
Everything is not.
Don't be fooled by the long line.
It's long because it hides big things.
You're not being told. You're playing hide and seek
in a mysterious architecture.
The long poem of concealment.
Everything hidden in the light.
Come here come here
Something I mean you to overhear

il maoismo (1971)

I don't remember writing these poems. Or why. By the vaguely apocalyptic tone of the title I imagine that they had something to do with paranoia about China's nuclear bombs and about the Bay Area Maoists one ran into on the streets. I'd moved to San Francisco in 1970 and I spent a lot of time in Chinatown, which may have led to some dreams or nightmares with Chinese motifs. Some of the poems seem plucked from dreams and it could well be that I'd had one of my periodic fits of "write-a-poem-every-morning-note-dream," which lasted for a week maximum (at a time). Oh, yes, and our mailman on Lowell Street was definitely Chinese.

As for the Maoists (none of whom were Chinese as far as I could tell), I hated them because their sanctimonious "revolutionary" bullshit reminded me of the brain-dead commissars back home in commie Transylvania. When I put together my next collection of poems, I doubtlessly left out this "Mao" cycle (with one exception) because I was afraid that some of my readers might think that I was actually FOR the guy when, clearly, the poems were all about how the guy gave me nightmares. Back home where I was born, we had a portrait of Stalin hanging over my crib.

Ironically, more than half a century later, in July 2005, I stayed in San Francisco in a house on Green Street with a portrait of Mao by Andy Warhol over my bed. I told my hostess, "One nightmare and the fucker is outta here!" She laughed and said, "Sure, move him if you like." I didn't have any nightmares, since it was a portrait by Andy Warhol, and was filtered through Andy's ironic view and thus rendered impotent.

The full import of the irony came home when James Mitchell came to visit me and handed me the July 1972 issue of *Sebastian Quill* No.3, the gay poetry magazine he edited in those days. There, in full mimeograph splendor, was my cycle of poems "Il Maoismo!" I read them in wonder and pointed out the Warhol connection. It was a week filled with coincidences, actually, a dense patch of meta-butterflies, so I took this to be just a silver glimmer among others. I seem to have been fond of "cycles" back then and while I used orthography minimally I was too insecure to completely dispense with it. I was also wrestling with the lower case "i," which looked better if every other noun was demoted. Presently, I lower-case most everything with the exception of the "I," and other arbitrary or momentary inflations, I've lost my false instrumental modesty.

—BATON ROUGE, AUGUST 12, 2005

climate

Around us, Mao, lies
an uncreated black, a face in which
all the uniform lines move to a ceaseless
military call. On the warm map
the eggs of the small countries roll
in a warm light.
The bottles on the windowsill
are half empty with the crosses in my
future sucking the liquid
with a pink straw. And this is
China through rose-colored glasses.
Later when the songs explode
I like you, Mao

a tool

This is the cradle
inside which new york, hong kong, and peking
squeeze with a shriek
to fuse into the
corporate baby. Who has, again,
fooled the jews and is running
upstream. Mao shears sheep
and grins in wait.

at the end of the world

At the end of the world holding a candle
or swimming in a box
under a clothesline, a little
red book floats to the surface
and in a flash of declining fishlight
we are both made inheritors
of the world
and into ashes. At which
cross in time the reflections of China
get their reward
in dreams. And a line of beds shakes
on a sloping smile.

an appraisal

i shall call all my past "mao"
and trail from tragedy to tragedy like a horse
in some interminable woods
following the noise of that clogged bathroom sink.
mao, your tragedy is the unfinished love
that follows you like a chopped snake.
a wake of flutes and morning in tangiers.
someone with a white sheet sells razor blades to girls.
all the little towns are in the background
of what's about to take place.
your heart is still inside the stiff tube
and in the choir of the neighborhood church
the beautiful boys are multiplying according to
forgotten angelic laws.
i leave this bowl of beans on your threshold
and this bundle of chills.
a future body looms at the windows
trying to open now one, now another.
who wants to grow up in this place?
i'm leaving all to the arriving event

a mao poem with bishop

I could get some help if I ever wanted it
from the Bishop who is tall
and has my welfare at heart.
Or from the Devil who is very small
and smells like a fart.
Or I can ask Mao
to lend me a goblin wet hand from the inside
of his cool caves to the inside
of my warm gizzard. What took
over me. Weird, I woke up thinking
that I need help. And now
I need it.

fingersnapping with mao

"Everything comes out of the barrel of a gun." —Mao

Revolution! Eels! Smashed windows! Ovulations!
A background put together for the purpose
of entering your world
with bayonet precision.
The peasants are boarding their windows.
Very soon the only clean faces left in the world
will be ours, and the wind
at the wheel.
Out of your gun come ashy birds and bats.
There is inside you something small and mean
vibrating like a feather, untranslatable.
It feeds on my refrains, on my repetitions,
on my clumsy deliveries of regulation uniforms
to desert guides,
it feeds more than it loves. I snap
my fingers in your face.
The fountain of your lifeseed spills in the bad soup.
Behold the spread vistas
in your metal eyes

mao's menu & jesus

Fat red lobsters
rolled in oil.
Ivy salads in gold rice.
A small bay tree
in the vinegar of this holy mountain.
The river
chases reindeer.
Mao eats.
The Son of God eats.
I count my prisons.
Each one with the time
and the birth of his crops.

when the summer is over

In the warm air a flippant recurrence
keeps Mao and me dreaming about
the end of the summer. Behind us we hear
our mutual translators, tongue to tongue,
knee to knee like neatly piled lumber
waiting for the main wall to go up.
But there is nothing either one of us would like
translated. It's been
a miserable summer. The wall
is not real. Only the tragic eggs
deposited by the sea in his cap have a hardness
against which I brace.
Waiting for the end of summer
we will tear off each other's music, Mao,
until the bleached bones fly free.
The waves shatter as we drown mutual insects
in the ripples of our communion

the end of mao

The last man at the Supper goes out for some more water
to keep the miracles going but the well
is muddy and the whorehouse across the way
blinks fresh lights at his breeches.
Every day, he thinks, is a day for miracles
but some days I grow dim. As an old poem says:
"there is a wig between my behavior
and my phenomena, and it's falling apart"
Die, Mao. The man stabs Jesus like an old boot.
For you, he says,
the language of affection does not starve itself
nor do the lights of well-fed poems
flicker to near extinction.
You're safe like a carpet of thorns inside
a language that knows only itself.
If we meet again it will be during a hunt
or in the middle of a flaming orchestra
tuning new instruments

morning

sometimes when they shut off the faucets
i think of the Chinese mailmen
how they must feel holding
birds full of letters.
i would like to walk with them
into the small
circumcisions at the top of houses
through which hands protrude waiting
for telegrams.
because this is a country of telegrams
we emerge from holding shocked doorknobs
between our knees

some poets

god tolstoy

well geez he came out of self-flagellation
with short whips made of green question marks
saying well geez over and over
like russia in lithographs fat ruddy men in dachas
glowing with healthy minerals strontium
until he knew beyond doubt that the geez
he launched into the wonder of it all
was addressed to himself and no one else
although in their tonic stinging the green
question marks woke up a slew of pronouns
like itches starting up serially from one mosquito
and spread through at least thirteen of his bodies
until his whole world itched but still it was his
body full of closets dachas full of ruddy men etc
he could squint and multiply the world by thousands
of himself who needs mirrors when you have a beard
and he could find no place to lean on except his beard
he was tolstoy exhausted having just written russia
now needing to use the immense scratcher he had been given at birth
by fairies who could see just what a stack of papers rose from the baby
and what stacks he was going to give birth to circling the earth
from siberia to cambridge mass and many places in many languages
here is your scratcher tolstoy dude and a white linen shift scented with hay
well, geez, well, geez, the world's on fire and I have a box of eternal values
I need to get to it's in a safety box at the metaphor bank in lausanne
have you seen the banker who can write me the go-ahead memo
a beard is a hard place to lean on oh geez oh jeez each beard-hair a war

russian poem

for marina tsvetaeva

in archetype world everything is cool
a nymph with glacial good intentions puts aside
her puppet of cinders and fortune cookies
and brings you a bubble of forgotten time
from around age six when she first got her doll
and points out the new tender skin around the bubble
and you proceed to lick it and palpate it softly
until it puts on another skin and another
to look eventually like a russian natasha wrapped in furs
gliding on her sled into the minds of future readers
leaving behind her a sparkling trail of easter eggs and sex hormones

the trouble starts when they slip into history
from the steep slope of an event natasha could not have foreseen
her mink boots were warm and inside one of them a toe was itching
the toe called boris pasternak
she being cultural had named all her toes after poets
(my favorite was lily brik the small one on her left foot)
and then she was barefoot and nude
no sled no clothes part of a gray huddle wobbling forward
the march of history
no jasmine scents from paris or even pastries from the street
no more pastries though the street (she assumed) was still there
her toes frozen in the snow and even though she couldn't feel them
she stubbornly remembered their names

that kind of stubborness the stubornness of a little princess
will save russia in the end (she thought)
and maybe it did
so history starts all over again
just when you feel safe and warm inside your fabergé egg
behind it's all boots and polished gun metal
and she can't look behind for fear of a bullet
the knut was childplay by comparison
climbing forward on the ice is not easy
hand over hand thought over matter

carbon gods come diamonds

MARINA TSVETAEVA (1892-1941) was born in Moscow, lived in exile in Berlin and
Prague, returned to Russia in 1938 where she was forbidden to publish. In 1941 she commit-
ted suicide, the traditional farewell of Russian poets, see Sergei Yesenin and Vladimir
Mayakovsky. Tsvetaeva was one of a constellation of Russian women whose work and lives
keeps shining: mentioned in this poem is also LILY BRIK, "the muse of the Russian avant-
garde" (Pablo Neruda), lover of Mayakovsky and sister of Elsa Triolet, the wife of Louis
Aragon—and so do the luminous strings of poetry tangle about us.

tristan tzara

for kenneth koch

sensibility was not what spelled doom
but rather forelocks and insouciance *palabras y cadavros*
the toasts made ten years before in a cocteau moment
fodder for a study of laughter using recordings
of the very first chortle of a chaplin audience
a child before a bicycle in the teens of the twentieth century
an hysteric before a psychiatrist a milestone guffaw
heard in the background the therapist hiding it with a cough
smiles hidden in photographs that had to wait decades
before the cost of film allowed printing hints of frivolity
beneath the victorians and edwardians' furrowed brows
below the severe bosoms trapped in steel concentration
smirks of spontaneity stashed behind duration's beams
a pause held too long and the devil's tail sneaks furry under the nose
of the orator's wife holding her first-row seat like a raft
next to her a daughter is being tickled by an angel with an erection
the only something in her capable of strangling the guffaw
is seeing her father dead after killing her mother and herself telling
this to a therapist with a pipe in a chair made of carved human hands
in let's say 1913 when a Jewish boy fresh out of the ghetto of Moineşti
could laugh suddenly irrepressibly in a concentrated burst releasing
centuries of repression and fear combined with a strict alphabet
leaving no airy gaps for sprigs of springtime rather light in frolic blooming
and did so on tape the cost be damned the drummer drums the centuries fly
recognition of something new following as surely as a peasant's gasp

before the nude legs of a mannequin being dressed in a shop by a widow
whose white ankles signal the death of acquired ancestral gloom
even as war rages all around and her killed husband rises in white forgetting
that is a laugh we must recover not for study but for feeling
what we know followed because tzara didn't laugh long enough
and we didn't laugh long enough with him are not now are we laughing

TRISTAN TZARA, a.k.a. Samuel Rosenstock (1896–1963) was a Romanian-born poet and essayist who founded Dada, the art movement that keeps on chugging, overshadowing the spectacular body of his poetry. I am writing a long essay/fantasy about a famous chess game between Tzara and Lenin in 1916 when they both lived in exile on the same street in Zurich. James Joyce also hung out at the same café, La Terrasse. All three were characters in Tom Stoppard's play, *Travesties,* but that particular chess game waits for me. In our time Dada is dead, long live Dada!, but Leninism is sure deader than dead, and no prols can cobble it back together again.

the incoming sneeze or the old man's nose
self-portrait

cranky old man looking more and more like the devil
in the caricature of a jew by an anti-semite
what are you doing by the pool of anger
with the rotating dresden doll in the black water
and the greek satyr painted on the wine jug
from which you take long sips and then sigh
wiping your mouth with a banana leaf
what up old cat staring into the bottom of your heart
a nose with a flower in it on the verge of a sneeze
you're holding back because you've been told that a revolution
may break out any second and you don't want to annihilate
the combatants with your powerful sneeze and so miss it
even though you know too damn much to romanticize any of that
still nobody can stop you from making trouble
overthrowing the government or any such trick
from your overstuffed bag of poesy snakes gathered on the roads
sucked from the deep seas vacuumed out of dreams
oblique is no more your style than sliced filets of suburban midnight
for you there is always beauty
you can recognize by a whiff like a perfume in a crowd
that's what your crooked nose is for
the effort is great but held in the suspense of your sneeze
worlds pass don't forget to squirt perfume into the air of the malthusian age

desk 07 in the reading room at the british library
june 19, 2003

marx and engels write the communist manifesto at the next desk
       08
    while at 06
bram stoker is looking over transylvania
    in a book
THIEVES OPERATE IN THIS ROOM
    above my leather desk 07

lenin at 05
    is penning communiqués
his application for a reader's card
    under the name jacob richter
has been approved yesterday
and it will end in the permanent exhibit
at the british library
being viewed by andrei and laura codrescu
    "richter!" muses laura, "like the scale."
jacob richter who will cause a large magnitude earthquake
    in the world

(in the czech republic a few days hence
    the couple is met by a student named geiger
born after the velvet revolution that undid lenin's earthquake
    many millions of dead people later)

and a new name is born out of the still-heaving womb of the 20th century:
    geiger richter
a radiation reader who detects seismic activity)

the "memory and mind" exhibition
    at the british museum (until September 23, 2003)

    marx and engels go to the pub
        (they've had a good day on the manifesto)
where they admire the bartender jenny
    karl marx's future wife
        to whom he is already penning
dreadful love poems he is careful to hide from engels
    frau engels expects the men for dinner
        she is fuming the roast is dry
they've been at the pub for six hours
    imagining the future
"the future my ass!" explodes frau engels, "it's that jenny, isn't it!"

    bram stoker goes walking on hampstead heath
        with a boner for lucy
who is already succumbing
           in his mind
to the transylvanian count
    he has just imagined

the future will include jenny and frau engels only for a little while
    and the marxian utopia and the vampire
will go on a long while

the marxian future fails spectacularly after two-thirds of a century
but the Vampire keeps chugging along far from spent into another millenium

THIEVES OPERATE IN THIS ROOM

how true
thieves among whom are future-burglars
     a.k.a. poets
          imagination workers
poor young in love with waitresses
     and virtuous corruptible lucys
too shy to ever steal anything physically
     not afraid on the other hand
         to break into the future
           & clean it out
without as much as an apology to us
     heirs and victims of utopia
     and vampires

time-thieves and widow-makers
     quietly penning verses

let us now praise a famous fool

for james hillman

possessed by several urgencies
the most urgent one
being old age
the old man set out to write his last book
a cri-de-coeur that would give the philosophy
he'd spent a lifetime upholding
(namely the archetypes of carl jung adjusted
to american life and its wealth of examples
as well as new archetypes such as elvis
who together with some new emotions such as embarassment
[to round out terror and pity]
the basis of his corpus
that made him a decent living from the wishes
of the no-longer-young hoping that there be deities
to answer for and order what may have been one or many mistakes)
an elegant simplicity testamentary and lucid
that expressed in moving sentences of sometimes inspired poetry
that in the irrational where dwelt the gods
the strongest of them War had lit a flame in whose heat
the truths of noble virtue sparked as bright as they did
in the idealized ancients who had themselves come out of books
(the old man having never gone to war himself
but dreamt it like a good poet of sorginte homerico
a good student and a fine hunk of a man fit for the company
of swiss and other aspiring aryans of the eranos)

and in this last book he succeeded both in discrediting
and lauding his masters like them or unlike them baring the veins
of classical fascism still visible in the corpse of europe
and sadly useless in america except as one of many snake oils
for the desperate but fickle students who had already run
to the biochemical cure at the first sound of any research trumpet
and in his chef d'oeuvre he revealed simplicity of heart as well
and good prose and some terror at having been all wrong
and in last gasp of the breathy fake sincerity
that had served his business well he proposed that art
a.k.a. eros stand up to ares by dispensing the sangre and virtu
intensely and straight out of the unconscious
to the kitsch-prone mass whom only War might ennoble

oh poor old man
a life a philosophy
gone to naught
betting on art
to not be caught too late
too late

JAMES HILLMAN, born 1926, is the foremost writer in English on Jungian psychology. He trained with Carl Jung in Zurich (this city keeps coming up!) and, while I have read his other works with admiring but wary delight, as you can see I had quite a violent reaction to his book, *A Terrible Love of War* (2004).

legacy: letters

"j'ai lu tous les livres mais la chair est triste, hèlas"
—paul valéry

"I would like to read, but where are the books?"
—mircea cărtărescu

quoting Valéry got you there every time
toltec submarine with dragonfly wings
mating with two or three of your kind on the wet ass
of the beloved floating downstream on a frog floatie
what a beautiful day to be dizzy with happy sun and shimmer
rock of brains built multicolorfully vertical for hawks to cruise
we make days by hand with the aid of god and her trembling fabric
fanfare of buzzing world of slinking lights breaking up in things
to unquote quotes and unmatter matters
surrender at the "hélas" yes we believe that we have
read all the books or that at least we didn't have to
since one who has read them all found in them
nothing better than them & that's as good
as having read them or what else are books for
and I the speaker am not that one but I know her
there is no contest between the them of books
and the them of the flesh we exalt now
a day like this intervenes and all that we knew escapes
and it won't do to ask where it went

it went into things and escaped as small breaths
from the tiny mouths of rodents and frogs and narrow snake ones
or sank into the eyes of an unmoved fly on a leaf
who forgot how she got there
all she knew was that it was time to eat
and that something would soon come close enough
mmm tasty leaf of philosophy
nourishment for many generations
I see no bodies petitioning to embody:
is that a scholar or a fly?
When I was on the leaf books shot out of me
dark moist hélas!
I heard the hawks and wasps and heard songs
her tresses askew
forever mate of a moment in playful sun.
At sunset there was a brief lingering
a yellowing of former self poorly observed
a dimming of exuberance
a marker to put there for the next sunrise
not "a definitive fall" to quote another someone.
The urge to go on dragged-out as a soldier is almost as good as sleep.
Believers in iridescent scarab mystery
report news of colors of seasons from old temperate forests
or cities where bricks with bat faces look out on executioners' squares.
A package of their letters smelling like coffee and smoke
is waiting for you at your mail drop in the next town.
Oxygen from mountaintop caves hisses in spirals down to the rooftops
filling with ardor the absentminded students kissing the bark of each other.
The bonbon spheres mix bouquets of evening with wafts of bistro
there is war somewhere but in here no fifth column
the paranoia of knowing oneself having subsided to give way for love,

solid pink, integrity like a cloud in a blue drink,
the shape of the urban future of our city written in lavender ink
on the faces of lovers sparking in starry beds,
tiny demon faces infused with crimson laughter.
See how pretty we dressed the questions up tonight!
I primped the exclamation points and hair-combed the commas
even as children were making rather stark movies about modern times
about themselves and their parents behind the cardboard trees.
I shook the powdered wigs under buggy lanterns
flakes of satire fell
and coleoptera simulating transparency
abrutum tendrae philtrae marstenicum saltunt
(so plant the brutish filter in the arsenic marsh).
Bruitism is a noisy art dead from the city,
an art we invented so that something might speak
when no one will be listening.
My love, I taught you gilded syllables
for the maggoty carnival,
collaboration creaking in its joints begging oil
for its most exquisite corpses,
phosphorus flesh flowing out of bars like piss into gutters.
But that was long ago when I embraced
the metaphorical and the literal under one wobbly streetlight
and cartoon corpses marched under the batons of candor and libido
to a text party like they used to give in the last century.
Now I'm with the fertile and the embodied
And this scattering of text paginating itself for the show
has already marked the moment
now please step out of the way
to make room for people coming in for drinks.
The trapeze has gone off shooting the remaining fools into the sky.

That would be us and the sunrise will be real not tequila.
Hélas so does art trim ranks and teeth
a steady rain on sidewalks and bartops.
That swoosh? The leather wings of generations migrating.
Is it fall already?

MIRCEA CĂRTĂRESCU, quoted often in this book, is a poet and novelist born in 1956 in Bucharest, Romania. His dense, poetic prose is a challenge to translators, but his book *Nostalgia* was splendidly rendered into English by Julian Semilian.

bicycle

for raymond queneau

touch that spoke while it spins
at the world exhibition in paris as all
the characters of sentimental novels
who have fled their masters' manuscripts
with morcol the detective of shadows
in hot pursuit being recorded by m. queneau
are mounting the bicycle seat one by one
and deciding their destinies in a fulgurant second
the appeal and the description by later
exegetic apologists for the postmodern
takes longer than we thought and besides
nobody dares touch the spoke as the wheel
spins not even the talented ones whose hands
have been slapped by something we'll call
culture or hypnosis or techno-somnolence
meanwhile time flies and nobody's having fun.

RAYMOND QUENEAU (1903-1976), French poet and novelist, cofounded OULIPO, Ouvroir de littérature potentielle, and was the only member of both the French Academy and the Pataphysical Academy. OULIPO's only American member is Harry Mathews.

ode

fifty years from the publication of howl
allen ginsberg in 1956 in san francisco
the abyss looked back but the young were
not frightened they leapt into the mouth
of the future and it wasn't hell like the elders
said but awesome sweat of youth mixed
with hellish light driven by spilled blood
history not the same one that pulled naomi
in its undertow and my people too
1956 was much closer to 1942
than 2006 and do we know anything more
yes we know joy and the pleasures of peace
as kenneth koch so aptly put it civilized
the mouth of hell wide-open
keeps howling through the ipods but its force
is parcelled and possibly diminished
allen you called it and it called you
we were your visitors even when you visited us
and visiting you did everyone remembers
in prague in baltimore and in new delhi
this addition of happiness your work
(fifty years' worth for everyone forty for me)

birds pecking
for philip lamantia

oh philip lamantia the occult whirled you away
to see robert duncan you have a few things to say
to each other finish the sentences you never
finished over the decades of fog and sun and bay
leaf and espresso and certainties so thin and sharp
they were made by gillette from odin's best coke
your eyes were pools of sympathy I couldn't look
into them very long I got vertigo the sutro park
vertigo the same sage-wrapped inevitability falling
through space looking over at seal rock from
somewhere near diana the huntress worshipped
apparently by others there were always offerings
at her feet where squirrels and birds came to eat
as they did around you and your beloved st. francis
sayonara philip lamantia us birds still pecking
at your verses will still do so for a brief while
do innocents exist

PHILIP LAMANTIA, discovered in tender youth by André Breton, practiced surrealism and alchemy in San Francisco, and was an indefatigable talker and researcher of mysteries. My favorite among his many books, *Bed of Sphinxes: New and Selected Poems, 1943-1993* (1997).

old poet

for sam abrams

the most imposing door
I have ever known a poet to have
across the street from St. Mark's Church
was opened by the namesake
of sam's novel
barbara herself
and I found myself at twenty years of age
a longhaired romanian
in the home of the greatest
new yorker possible as if all that
eastern european jewish immigration
for the past one hundred years
had been for a very good purpose indeed
and when later I embarked on my education
by looking up the poetry classes
at the old courthouse on 2nd avenue
I settled for joel oppenheimer's instead
of sam abrams's because quote
in sam's class you have to smoke a joint
before class even starts unquote
i'm not sure who said that
maybe michael stephens who attended
sam's class though maybe just for the pot
but pot made me very nervous
still does

but hail the pot poet he's wise still
and you can get high just saying his name
sam abrams from new york poet

the zen post office
for pat nolan

at the zen post office no letters
being sent or received the people
wander in to ask is this the zen
post office and other people there
just to hang out say yes at once
everyone sits down on the windows
where normally clerks stamp
there are no stamps to lick
take a seat by the wanted poster
some of us are writing letters
to people no longer among us
or people we never met or just
invented or are hoping to meet
when they are invented by others
but nothing is being sent plus
the people who look like they are
reading just-received communiqués
are simply looking over at what
is being composed by others
the whole city is like that now
heat and uselessness are drivers
of men and women's wombs

one day I decided to go to work
at the *la vie en rose café*

97

the place smelled like sun lotion
and the locals were taking coffee
with cream lots of cream
until noon the café was a sea
of reports and poems being filed
by the waves made by legs being crossed
and recrossed and restless sandaled feet
and newspapers self-importantly creased
items torn noisily out for later
and sudden boys and girls reciting menus
with great concentration and eyes closed
in various accents castilian and welsh among them
the news was dire the menu had not improved
despite the addition of several imported herbs
the sunbathing beauties at the shores of the urban sea
were too far to be seen and too exhausting to imagine
but there was an orchestra across the street
and I was writing it all down with a view to mailing it
from the zen post office above the café
its marine glory as incommunicado as its sister universe

PAT NOLAN, born in 1944 in Montréal, is a poet of the California Zen school, a master of understatement, irony, and a deep understanding of nature. His many limited edition books and broadsides are a delight for the dedicated few who love his work. This poem is a flash-back to the early 1970s when I lived in Monte Rio, California, where Pat Nolan, Jeffrey Miller, myself, and other poets lived through a memorable and dramatic time.

who's afraid of anne waldman?

On the occasion of the Anne Waldman Symposium,
Ann Arbor, Michigan, March 13, 2002

I talked about Anne before I even met Anne
      In 1967 in the fall
A year after I came to America
Alice and I hitchhiked from Detroit
      To New York and stayed
On 125th Street in Harlem with a couple named Allegra & Jack
      Allegra had been Lewis Warsh's girlfriend
         Before Lewis met Anne
& when I showed Allegra my poetry she said:
"you must show these to Anne Waldman,"
& what I thought she said was:
"You must show these to Walt Whitman"
      not really, but
         Allegra was naked at the time
& sitting on Jack's lap with the sheaf of my poems
      in her hand
& I was so startled by that
      I dropped the two cans of soup I had just stolen
         from the corner store
which I thought was pretty bold,
      but so was this way of looking at poetry.
Alice & I went back to Detroit for the riots
      & it was another year before I met Anne—but

first I met Ted Berrigan
       who was teaching a poetry class at the Old Courthouse on 2nd Avenue
       (The teaching of poetry in those days was serious business!)
I ended up hanging by Gem Spa at the corner of 2nd Ave & St. Mark's
       Place
       with Ted's disciples
& I became one too, I guess
       when I saw that he could overcome just fine
       in content and voice volume
       his competition
            Ben Morea the Motherfucker
who used the same corner for starting riots
on weekends
       with the lovely slogan:
"Free Food! Free Food down at the graveyard!"
       which was the graveyard at the St. Mark's Church
where Peter Stuyvesant is buried
       and should be dug up
so we can put Ted Berrigan there instead
       —from the Gem Spa radiated a vast array of activities
           carried out by mobs of agents of the esprit
              du temps
cadre of longhaired cappeloni brimming with inexact missions
       all filled with light delights revolutionary zeal
           & occasionally paranoia & terror
though in 1968 the summer of love in New York
       the delight was much denser than paranoia

& I followed Ted around for about two weeks
       until he looked at my poems
       & the next thing I knew
       I was invited to 33 St. Mark's Place
       across the street from Gem Spa

& here was the literary heart of the lower east side
which was the Number 1 bohemia in the world in 1968
with London a distant 2nd
and San Francisco on its way out

Anne Waldman & Lewis Warsh in residence

Publishers of *The World*

The mimeo monthly of the St. Mark's Church in-the-Bowerie
Poetry Project
Anne Waldman director

33 St. Mark's Place was the inner sanctum
the command bunker of the New York School of Poetry
manned by the second generation

who coined that "second generation" business anyway?

At 33 St. Mark's Place
everyone was a poet
we conducted circular missions
wide circles that touched
on other circles
of painters & musicians
& Andy Warhol's crowd
all the way uptown to Lita Hornick's
& to the Hamptons
& vertically in time to other bohemias
that had just gotten tired

absolutely nobody was ever tired at 33 St. Mark's Place

and amid this current & historic rebel splendor
        was Anne cool classical beautiful
energetic, intelligent & in charge

everyone was in love with her
        it was the summer of love Anne Waldman

there wasn't anybody who didn't love Anne Waldman
        except the Establishment didn't love any of us
            but even the Establishment
        if we had let the Establishment
            anywhere near us
would have loved Anne Waldman

but Anne Waldman didn't love the Establishment
        she was a "Dark Commando"

"private property that's why
you can't snuggle up to someone else's trees"

        and she went to the store to buy:

1. PRINCE fast drying RUBBER CEMENT
2. air-mail envelopes
3. brown wrapping paper
4. a light-blue washcloth

and declared these things "necessary to my daily life / as love sex
happiness joy"

now there was a Pop credo
        there was faith
            there was a hood

as in the next breath she thought about her friends, "Martha in Vermont," "Ted in Maine," and "all the people everywhere in the country / surrounded by trees / &water&birds&the song of the birds / heard in our land / America America America,"

quite breathlessly

and if you went back to that list you'd find that the Rubber Cement was for glueing Allen Ginsberg's poem "Wales Visitation" cut from the *New Yorker*, and her annoyance at people who use Elmer's

and from there to missing her friends
to total pantheism
& the pickle of American policy

there was only a wave of breath the same breath

Of course we were young
& we had a lot of breath

and a new mission that included
1. taking nothing for granted
&   2. making sure everyone was in love with you
&   3. vanquishing the masters of war
&   4. staying high
&   5. making a new art & literature

and amazingly
we accomplished all that

esp. 2 & 4

but when I met Anne I felt very young indeed
awkward

Ted seemed to me an ancient—he was at least 28
Dick Gallup—a man from centuries past—27 at least

And Anne
          Anne was only a year older than me
               But she was sophisticated
                 Elegant
         She was Olympian
Essence of cool
         Totally American
& all these New York poets who knew each other so well
         were also rich
or so it seemed to me still stealing cans from the A&P
         & deploying my accent

I'm still deploying that but I have a couple of credit cards now

These Americans scared me
         They were so American!
And Anne was the most American!
         She even put brand names in her poems!
Elmer's! The Mets! The *NY Times!*

I was brooding and seething with philosophy

but I had one thing over them
         my secret weapon
my belief that I had taken acid
         at least five months before anyone
in the New York School 2nd generation

This was my firm belief

At least until a month ago when I talked to Anne
       & we ascertained that yes, indeed,
I had taken acid in the spring of 1966 in Rome
       But that she was only a month or two behind

A difference that by 1968 meant nothing

Since by then we had all taken acid—

Still, there was this class thing—

      Bohemian pedigree
I never quite felt at home at 33 St. Mark's Place
       I thought that people were laughing at me
          They probably were
I made some jokes
       They weren't laughing at those

But I do feel home now at 33 St. Mark's Place
       Because Ted Berrigan wrote this:

It begins

"It's just another April almost morning, at St. Mark's Place
Harris and Alice are sleeping in beds; it's far too early
For a scientific massage, on St. Mark's Place, though it's
The RIGHT place if you feel so inclined."

and it ends:

"Calling right from where you are, in Anne's place,
As to your heart's delight, here comes sunlight."

I had one of my graduate assistants
    Go through Ted's complete works to find out
        How many times Anne's name appears in his poems:
        438 times!

Mine only appears twice

In 1968, 1969, 1970, 1971, 1972—my poems appeared in *The World*.
Not just one poem but many. And everyone on the scene had not
one poem but many in *The World*. We could appear as rich as we
wanted to be, knowing that the bar was set high, the standards quite
elevated. Culture.

    Anne Waldman was my publisher.
    Anne liked my poems.
    I know, maybe it was Lewis who REALLY liked my poems
    But I preferred to think that it was Anne who really really
liked my poems.

    The word "counterculture" had just come into vogue
A word I never liked
    Il s'agit of culture pure and simple
What's this *counter* all about?
    The counterculture had utilitarian aspects indeed
And insofar as we were rebel poets we were serving this counterculture
    By making joyous noises wherever we went
    And angry noises too, but joyously

The readings at St. Mark's place
At public meetings
At antiwar rallies
In the parks

Everything had a grand scheme like a big top over it

      But the New York poets were not like that
Well, some of them weren't

Ted was about as apolitical
        & pro-American as you can get
he wrote "fuck communism" and mentioned the passing parade
      because it was there
             not because he was against the war
in fact I never heard him mention it
but he got off on cheeseburgers
          both in poems and in life
      (when he could afford them)
and those attitudes & appetites drove the peaceniks & the vegetari-
    ans crazy

      so that this "counterculture" might have been catering to
some Big Ideas
but many of us poets still stole from the store

      even The Diggers' store
        which was "free"

& the appeal of the New York School in the Sixties
was precisely its apolitical feel
      that allowed that art is art only
        & only art

that it's not bombs or propaganda

      until that attitude became a propaganda of its own

      but that's another story

& the New York School was a refuge also for midwesterners and
finns and romanians and escapees of every sort even for some cate-
gories of people who had no I.D. tags yet

I would call this the apolitical stage of the New York School
        For those in the audience
Who know Anne's amazing activist career
        After 1970 or so
& first her vice-presidency of the Counterculture
        under President Ginsberg
& then her Presidency of the Counterculture
& while the personal was certainly political
        it was a lot more personal than political back then
we were just amazed to be alive at such an interesting time

& Anne was breathless and a busy bee

        publishing *The World*
                the St. Mark's readings
                        her own poems

& all the lives I knew nothing about—

the word "community" might mean more than "counterculture"
but I think that "family" fits better La Famiglia La Cosa Nostra
because we had some major ties & were up many nights writing
together & keeping up the dark shift until the radiators hissed
"Basta!"

there were so many people in this family
        I won't name names
because I am no longer a New York School poet
        I'm a New Orleans poet

first generation

The only way not to be in the New York School back then
　　　was to not want to be a New York School poet
　　　　　and to not know Ted or Anne

I remember Bill Knott reading a nasty poem about the New York School
　　　at St. Mark's Church one time
　　　he said "the New York school is a spigot on a corpse"
or some such thing & Ted shouted from the back of the room,
　　　"Bill, you can be in the New York School now!"

Anne & Ted wrote a poem together
　　　"Memorial Day,"
and it was such a great poem
we read it over and over
and many people still read it

it was a love poem to America & to all of us

a masterful collaboration
in a collaborative age and place
that was a small pool swarming with life
current & past life
from which sprang many streams
that are now flowing everywhere in America
stocked with all kinds of fish who had never
been born before 1967

Ted Berrigan was the Prime Mover
Éminence grise & Pink & White
And sometimes deus ex machina
But Anne was the Goddess Machina

She was the whole machine
The little engine that could
The Total Goddess of Work

& when she drove people too hard
they ran off to Poppa Ted and he severely critiqued their verses
& made them pay for the check

& then the members of the family
began dispersing, and making families
of their own, in Bolinas, in Colorado,
in San Francisco, in Jersey, and in England

but never forgetting to pay tribute to Anne
& send their poems to *The World*
& read at the Church at least once a year

At least I did—

Anne went on to inhabit two states
The State of New York
And The State of Colorado
States of Mind with buildings on them

"the community we are developing at Naropa
is already very strong
and continues as a webwork
extending into the planet at large"

The planetary business
The Allen Ginsberg business

"The new deeper voice
The poet's path
Voice and wisdom
The tough tongue of a crone"

All Anne's words

But also:

"Heady talk in La Garona restaurant after poetry show
Cathars argue separatism"

Anne's genius then as always
To give back in talk
What the world gave her in sound
Texture fact gossip and news

Intense talk
Thick with the density of various streams
Not just language hoping to win the lottery

The magnetized Olsonian field
Through which one travels
Gathering intensities

Throwing body and soul into the dance

Anne's New York family
Made alliances with other families
& there were great familial reunions
& great familial tragedies
& truly down moments
like the Naropa Poetry Wars

when Anne told me apropos of Tom Clark's
book about it:
"the family umbrella's shredding"

and that was such a fine Cold War metaphor
for all of us still under the atomic umbrella

but the family just kept getting bigger
with or without an umbrella
because Anne's interests got bigger

and there was a whole tent city
where the umbrella stood

And she became new Annes
Some of whom I knew some of whom I didn't
One Anne after another
I kept up with Anne in books

And once or twice a year in person

So I do know of Anne the Traveler
Anne the Dream Journalist
Anne the Raw-feeling Lyricist
Anne the Keeper of the Record
Anne the Epistolary
        —I have about a hundred cards scribbled by Anne,
        all of them ending, "Love, Anne"—
Anne the Naropa Builder
Anne the Shaman
Anne the Performing Shaman
Anne the Heavyweight Poetry Champion of the World in Taos
Anne the Teacher

Anne the Student
Anne the Flirt
Anne the Interviewer
Anne the Interviewee
Anne the Essayist
Anne the Historian
Anne the Mourner
Anne the Protester
Anne the Refusenik
Anne the Propagandist
Anne the Environmentalist
Anne the Gringa
Anne the Mother
Anne the Daughter
Anne the Founding Father
Anne the Witch
Anne the Buddhist
Anne the Feminist
Anne the Lover
Anne the Wife
Anne the Patient
Anne the Therapist
Anne-with-Allen Anne
Anne-in-Meetings Anne
Professional Anne
Amateur Anne
Rolling Thunder Revue Anne
Anti Mega-Mega Bomb Anne
Anne at West Point Anne

I heard about them
I read them

I do know Anne-in-stories Anne
I know what x, y, z said about Anne
And I've seen little Annes
Perform nationwide at slams
I know the I-am-a-little-scared-of-Anne Anne
I'm a little scared of Anne

But I'm not sure which Anne I'm scared of
Anne's always been a good friend to me
& that's Anne-my-friend Anne

and this is Anne—the List
Alpha-bibliographical Anne

"Kill or Cure" dreams nightmares
Congresses with the Muse the male/female personae
There is Iovis Anne
        Some scary dude
And the tractatus on the sentence of marriage
        Ten to life if you're not careful
Baby breakdowns & grown-up tantrums
        & the more I read the less I know Anne
In some of these books Anne is a state more than a person
        It's Anne-land
& you best go there in the summer

Anne-land is big
Is like Ginsberg-land
Or Yevtushenko-land
A regular country with seasons
& a foreign policy

relations with Italy and the Czech Republic are good

but since Heider Austria's not so hot

and I actually feel the pathos of a thousand readings
or performances a thousand late-night colloquia
the ocean of talk
the wordless chasms between faces

the ever-widening sea of humanity with its center
in Anne

Anne cannot be lost
that "vow to poetry" is to be ever-present
a tough job
& even Anne needs some sleep now and then

      I can identify with that

& with such magnitude comes a bedrock solitude
      I know about that
& the dead sometimes appear
      more alive than the living

being awake more natural than being asleep

"Listen to the fragmented buildings
and the decorum of traffic getting somewhere."

the dead fly in
      like big patching bees to patch the family umbrella

I think the idea of Ted as a big fat bee patching
      The family umbrella
          Is quite funny

& I can see Allen in that role, too,
with a big darning needle
        but others just hang out
        watching Ted & Allen work
& just shout "Go!"
I'm probably being unfair to a hundred of the hard-working dead
        Be kinder to the dead
        They work just as hard
        Anne, materialist and utopian,
                At times:
"They laid me out on the table all decked out,
scratched me with their metal & I bled &
they began sucking & eating. And you were the
last to partake & that was when I didn't care
anymore, love or hate. And you were going to
love me when we abolished hunger"

Note that this is utopianism
        Not merely in the service of ending hunger
But eternally hopeful of tasting good
        Even as a corpse

Love, Anne's major theme,
And work, her major praxis

In the tent city the young are hard at work

& Anne is Queen of the Young
while some of us as Ted once said to Tom Clark
are still just "majors in the army of the young."

Fielding Dawson, recently dead,
        Wrote in *House Organ* no.37

"the influence of the Hag in her performance art
       who I first witnessed at Naropa in 1978
              an unforgettable experience
       for I was seeing my mother before my very eyes."

It's not the first time Fielding saw his mother
       At a performance I'm sure
But Anne sure scared him

I did find Anne on stage pretty scary
       At the Taos Heavyweight Poetry Bout
       My money was on Anne
       I can't even remember who the challenger was
       He just wasn't fast enough
       For fast-talking woman
       The world gets faster it's a fact
       News from Hubble
       It's giving pause to the Big Bang Boys
       Who thought that the universe was taking it easy
       Post-Bang

And the longer we live
The more we know without speaking
We are standing
In a room full of ghosts
That's not scary
That's now

& when we stop standing
there will be shelves of us
standing for us

at the U of M

but not very well

Getting old is everyone's private business
Staying young is a collective affair
& it's nice to have a place for your papers

& so I sat with a stack of Anne's books by me
        opening them at random
        for some oracular clues to this
        wholly other kind of performance
        where Anne is at the center but not on stage
        which must be very unusual
        Forgive me for trying your patience, Anne

& I came up with this
(from "Kill or Cure"):

"put in:
commodities
put in new-found seas
put in courtesy & wit
put in symmetry
put in coffin cords & a bell
put in extreme breathing
put in a cosmic image
put in a feminine image
put in politics, brass-tacks level
put in how he was in love with Turkish eyes
put in this machine recording
put in like footprints of a bird on the sky
put in lifting arms embargo
put in where you are cherished
put in still a little bit up in the air,"

and I think that I put in a bit of all that, except for "the arms embargo," and maybe I didn't say anything—or too little—about being in love with Anne's Turkish eyes, but I certainly put in some extreme breathing and, I hope, some courtesy and wit. I mostly wanted to put in where she is cherished, because she is. I certainly put in "still a little bit up in the air," which is how I hope we stay this entire conference, though not off the wall or without feet on the ground.

in memory of the 20th century
for robert creeley

not innocence innocents
an unequivocal answer
could only come from an innocent
the guilty hedged their bets
yes those who believe
in the good intentions of others
are the innocents
and when evidence to the contrary
rises from institutes staffed by neighbors
or from their spawn or the newspapers or mail
they are sure that an error was made somewhere
the clerks of heaven are correcting it as we speak
and if they die unconvinced they return as visitors
to take revenge on their own naiveté and innocence
these are the saddest visitors of all

the tourist towns are strung like pearls
along the coasts and on the peaks
they thrum they glow in the minds of tourists
lugging an ocean of myth in brochures
heavy as mountains of longing
palm pilots full of internet sadness
churches cafés sex clubs on cliffs or caves
blood quickens in an agglomeration
of postcards of ancestors smothered

by desire to return ectoplasmatical and refashioned
from their old countries with advice and smoked sausages
full of idealized landscapes
they've cried enough enough in their saucy graves
they are back on a tidal wave of yearning
ready to sell the little kitschy things they made while dead
they are themselves tourists visiting their living descendants
who now take them home and hang them like flags from rafters
warning figures of continuity to bums without origin or any vagabond
who might mistake tourism for comedy or something local
or offer an insult in the form of money or some other rude crude
eventually the clan shreds and tatters fly (it is windy

present at the ceremony

art won
there wasn't even a contest
now art is on tv every time you turn it on
you used to say that art is the great enemy
and now it's true
there was a time when that sounded like a joke
made by an artist posed with a cigar between a neon sign for bar
and a monk moon
art is the greatest enemy another drink please
then swaggering home under the monk moon weeping
the technology of the cosmos arrayed itself predictably overhead
as art advanced in the dark on the backs of stealthy products
which entered the mouths of sleepers like serpents
in the morning everyone had strange appetites
they drove fantastic wombs to work and when they got there
work was a game and everybody was ready to play
I have swallowed my reptiles early the police made me do it
everybody else had to wait until the devices became user-friendly
and they put white smoke and sugar on the reptiles

Maelstrom: Songs of Storm & Exile
NEW ORLEANS KLEZMER ALLSTARS

Produced by the New Orleans Klezmer Allstars and Andrew Gilchrist
Lyrics ©2008 Andrei Codrescu

Jonathan Freilich, guitars
Glenn Hartman, accordion, piano
Nobu Ozaki, bass
David Rebeck, violin, viola, mandola, accordion on track 6
Dave Sobel, drums, percussion
Robert Wagner, clarinet, saxophone, piano on tracks 7, 15, 18

Recorded, tolerated, and mastered by Andrew Gilchrist at House of 100ohz, New Orleans, LA. Andrei Codrescu recorded by Jonathan Freilich at Yoganada, New Orleans, LA. Additional recording by: Christopher K, vocals on tracks 7, 10, 16, Seven Generations Studios, Forest Knolls, CA; Scott Beelman, vocals on tracks 2, 14, My Living Room, New Orleans, LA; Robert Wagner, additional clarinets, The Purple Place, Brooklyn, NY; Jonathan Freilich, track 11, Yoganada, New Orleans, LA; John Lawrence, vocal on track 20, Casa de Yanaê, New Orleans, LA; Andrew Gilchrist, piano on track 14, Helen's House, New Orleans, LA.

In Memory Cantor Stephen Dubov 1951–2006

This record made possible with a grant from B'nai Brith International. Thanks Adam Shipley and the Tipitina's Foundation. Special thanks to Andrei and everyone at Coffee House Press.

1 **Gone, but Forgotten** Composer, Robert Wagner; cello, Helen Gillet

2 **Stuck Here with My Goat** (from the poem "what to do with your goat . . ."). Composer, Robert Wagner; vocals, Coco Robicheaux

3 **Fiddler on a Cheap Blue Roof** Composer, Robert Wagner

4 **Bodies in the Flood** (from the poem "crepuscular (the family tomb)"). Composer, Alex McMurray; vocals, Alex McMurray; guitar, Alex McMurray; accordion, David Rebeck

5 **The Army, National Guard, NOPD and FEMA Tantz** (from the poem "looting walmart"). Composer, Robert Wagner; vocals, Andrei Codrescu

6 **Tale of Two Cities** (from the poem "tale of two cities"). Composer, Jonathan Freilich; vocals, Andrei Codrescu

7 **Married Men's Girlfriends** (from the poem "the breakups"). Composer, Robert Wagner; vocals, Valentina Osinski, John Kendall Bailey, and Andrei Codrescu; cello, Helen Gillet

8 **Bush Flies Over Laughing** Composer, Robert Wagner

9 **Fridges to Heaven** (from the poem "fridges to heaven"). Composer, Glenn Hartman; vocals, Andrei Codrescu

10 **Cleaning Ladies** (from the poem "cleaning ladies"). Composer, David Rebeck; vocals, Valentina Osinski

11 **Mother Quarter** (from the poem "mother quarter"). Composer, Jonathan Freilich; bass, Alex McMurray; vocals, Andrei Codrescu

12 **New Year in Cochin** Composer, Jonathan Freilich; clarinet, Chris Cole; bass, Dave Anderson

13 **FEMA Check** (from the poem "that fema check"). Composer, Glenn Hartman; vocals, Harry Shearer

14 **Molly's Window** (from the poem "from the window at molly's"). Composer, Glenn Hartman; vocals, Ivan Neville; tenor saxophone, Ben Ellman

15 **Mr. Mayor** (from the poem "the town meeting"). Composer, Robert Wagner; vocals, John Boutte; cello, Helen Gillet

16 **Mold Song** (from the poem "the mold song"). Composer, Jonathan Freilich; vocals, Valentina Osinski and John Kendall Bailey

17 **KatrinaKrewe** Composer, Robert Wagner

18 **Coffe House Philosophers** (from the poem "the coffee house philosophers"). Composer, Robert Wagner; vocals, John Boutte, featuring the New Orleans Happy Man's Choir

19 **.Kom** Composer, Rob Wagner

20 **Toma Tiempo de Realizar que Estas Muerto** (from the poem "new orleans limbo"). Composer, John Lawrence; John Lawrence, guitar; vocals, Chayito Champión

21 **Klez Hafez** Composer, Jonathan Freilich; clarinet, Chris Cole; baritone saxophone, Ben Ellman